Auto Scaling Group Desynchronization

Prevention & Resolutions

Table of Contents

Chapter 1. Introduction

Welcome to this Special Report, where we delve into the critical, yet often overlooked, issue of Auto Scaling Group Desynchronization. This comprehensive report is designed with deep insights to provide an understanding of this challenge, whether you're an experienced IT practitioner, a budding software engineer, or perhaps just technically curious. In our exploration, we will not only uncover the potential causes of desynchronization in auto-scaling groups, but also present preventive measures and practical resolutions. In this report, we enable readers to appreciate the importance of synchronization optimization, without the engagement of high-level jargon. This accessible and invaluable resource is your gateway to ensuring optimized, resilient, and seamless system operations within your realm.

Chapter 2. Understanding Auto Scaling Groups: Core Concepts

Auto Scaling groups (ASGs) are a service provided by cloud providers, such as Amazon Web Services (AWS), designed to manage the scalability, high availability, and redundancy of your workload in the cloud environment. They adjust server capacity in accordance with the actual demand and ensure that new instances take the place of any that are unavailable or underperforming.

2.1. Infrastructure of ASGs

The fundamental elements of an Auto Scaling Group are:

1. EC2 instances: The server units managed by the ASG. They can be of different types and capacities depending on the workload and demand.

2. Launch configurations: These contain information about which Amazon Machine Image (AMI) to use, the instance type, security groups, and any other settings you control for your instances.

3. Scaling policies: They define how the ASG should increase or decrease the number of instances. Policies can be simple (like maintaining a specific number of instances) or more complex and based on CloudWatch alarms.

4. Health Checks: The ASG uses these to determine the status of the instances. Healthy instances are kept running while unhealthy ones are replaced.

2.2. Understanding Scalability

Scalability is the ability of a system to handle an increase in workload. In ASG, this includes the ability to add or remove servers according to need, making the system highly flexible. Scalability can be:

1. Vertical: This involves increasing the capabilities (RAM, CPU, etc.) of an individual instance in response to increased demand.

2. Horizontal: This features the addition of more instances to distribute the load rather than increasing the capability of an individual instance.

In most cases, ASGs use horizontal scaling because it offers more flexibility and better cost management.

2.3. High Availability and Redundancy

High availability ensures that systems are continuously operational over a long duration, while redundancy is a measure taken to prevent failure of a system due to failure of a single component. An ASG provides both by automatically replacing failed or underperforming instances.

2.4. Costs and Efficiency

ASGs are more cost-effective since you only pay for the instances that are running. Cost also corresponds to the instance type and the region. Additionally, with services like AWS's EC2 Spot Instances and Reserved Instances, you can further optimize costs.

2.5. Task Scheduling

Task scheduling in ASGs can be timed or demand-based. You can schedule actions by specifying the date and time when the ASG should execute these actions. Alternatively, you can configure your group to scale based on demand by specifying scaling policies and observing metrics.

2.6. Understanding Desynchronization

In an ideal scenario, all instances within an auto scaling group should be running the same version of the application, synchronized with the same dataset. But occasionally, certain instances could get 'stuck' at an older version or fail to synchronize with the data source causing a desynchronization.

Instances could get into a 'stuck' state due to several reasons - stability issues in the application, timing out due to heavier workloads, spotty network connectivity, problems with the deployment process, etc. The result is inconsistent service, with some instances serving out-of-date content or functioning abnormally.

2.7. Addressing Desynchronization

Desynchronization can disrupt operations and lead to less optimized system performance. To address desynchronization, regular health checks, application and instance monitoring, efficient deployment processes, robust networking and improved application stability are strongly recommended.

In conclusion, understanding the core concepts of Auto Scaling Groups forms the basis for effective management of systems and applications. They offer critical benefits of scalability, high availability, cost efficiency and more, though these features bear their own complexities, such as desynchronization, which must be properly managed to ensure optimal system performance.

Chapter 3. The Essence of Synchronization in Auto Scaling Groups

Auto scaling groups (ASGs) have emerged as an indispensable approach to accommodating the volatile load that is associated with a myriad of application types. This technology leverages the elasticity of cloud platforms, instantiating and terminating instances based on actual load conditions rather than projected demands. The result is a more cost-effective and resource-efficient solution that maintains robust system performance even during load surges.

However, despite the immense potential and proven utility, the perspective of synchronization within an ASG is often sidelined, leading to the potential emergence of what we term as 'Auto Scaling Group Desynchronization.' An understanding of synchronization within an ASG and the potential for desynchronization is essential for the successful deployment and maintenance of an ASG.

3.1. Understanding Synchronization in ASGs

The concept of synchronization can be best understood by picturing an orchestration in which each musician is an instance within the ASG. For the symphony to work cohesively, each instrument needs to be in sync - playing the correct note at the right time. Similarly, each instance within an ASG must flawlessly perform its duties in accordance with the rest of the group for the application to function correctly. This synchronization refers not merely to the tasks performed by the instances but also to the state of the instances themselves.

Instances within an ASG are dynamic. They are created and decommissioned following the scalability policies defined. This continual fluctuation can result in new instances not having the same state as existing instances, leading to a discrepancy in data, configurations, or workload status. It is these differences, or the lack of synchronization, that form the focal point of this examination.

3.2. The Impact of Desynchronization

Desynchronization might not seem like a major concern. After all, ASGs do their most crucial job — bringing up and tearing down instances — effectively. However, such a notion stems from a somewhat narrow perspective that ignores the potential implications of inconsistencies across instances.

First and foremost, an out-of-sync ASG can cause partial or even complete application failures. As instances within an ASG share workload, inconsistencies across them could lead to inconsistent application behavior, causing service disruptions or failures.

Secondly, diagnostic and troubleshooting become increasingly challenging with desynchronization. Since an inconsistency might not be easily repeated, linking it with a particular instance becomes a formidable task.

Lastly, the absence of synchronization leads to inefficient utilization of resources. An instance that is not properly synced with others may end up repeating tasks or underutilizing its resources, leading to wastage.

3.3. Preventive Measures Against Desynchronization

Prevention, as they say, is better than cure; the rule holds equally true for Auto Scaling Group Desynchronization.

For starters, designing stateless instances can dramatically reduce the chances of desynchronization. In a stateless design, instances do not hold any user data or session information, making the influence of one instance on the overall application minimal. This independence means that bringing up a new instance or tearing down an existing one doesn't disrupt the state of the ASG.

Another effective strategy is the usage of Lifecycle hooks in ASGs. Lifecycle hooks ensure that before an instance is put 'InService' or before it is terminated, certain customized actions are executed, thus ensuring all instances are in the desired state before they actively join or leave the group.

Applying configuration management tools can also alleviate issues. Tools like Ansible, Chef, or Puppet can ensure that new instances are created with the correct configuration and that existing instances can be updated to reflect state changes. Using such a tool strengthens the degree of synchronization within an ASG by maintaining consistent configurations across all instances.

One should consider employing Immutable Infrastructure, where once an instance is deployed, it never gets upgraded or updated. Instead, if a change is required, a new instance is created with the desired state. This approach ensures that the state of all running instances remains consistent, which reduces the possibility for desynchronization.

3.4. Practical Resolutions when Desynchronization Occurs

However much we try to prevent, there may be situations when we encounter desynchronization. In such scenarios, it is crucial to have a process in place to restore synchronization across the instances in the ASG.

To begin, ensure that you have robust and regular health checks in place. Setting up scripts and monitoring services to periodically check if the instances are in sync with one another can help spot instances that have veered off course. Once you have detected an inconsistent instance, it can be marked as 'Unhealthy' and terminated, causing the ASG to spin up a new instance in return, which, with the right preventive measures, should be in sync with the rest of the group.

Moreover, invest in real-time monitoring and alerting tools. This combination ensures that changes in the state of an instance that could lead to desynchronization are caught in real time, allowing for immediate corrective action before the discrepancy expands.

Backup systems can also come in handy. With an appropriate backup strategy, restoring an instance to the appropriate state, or sourcing a new instance, can be expedited.

To summarize, an ASG's optimal functionality is imbued with a major dependency on the synchronization across its instances. Despite the negligence this perspective usually receives, understanding and maintaining synchronization within an ASG is paramount. Equipped with the right understanding, preventive measures, and action plans can stave off potentially significant failures or inefficiencies and ensure smoothly functioning, optimized applications.

Chapter 4. Potential Causes of Auto Scaling Group Desynchronization

Auto Scaling is a controller service that manages the operator lifecycle, by automating system scaling based on specific metrics, ensuring infrastructure resilience during peak loads or failures, and maintaining efficiency during off-peak periods. However, when an Auto Scaling Group (ASG) drifts into a desynchronized state, it can disrupt these functions and pose significant challenges in the operational landscape, necessitating protracted troubleshooting and mitigation efforts.

4.1. The Concept of Auto Scaling Group Desynchronization

Auto Scaling Group Desynchronization, in essence, occurs, when the actual state of the system diverges from its expected state. This discrepancy can occur in various aspects, such as the number of running instances, the CPU utilization, or the response rate of the auto-scaled service.

In a synchronized ASG, the real-time health status, metrics, and operations align accurately with the anticipated configuration specifications. However, when discrepancies arise, leading to the instances' inconsistent status, resource allocation inefficiencies, or unanticipated fluctuations, we refer to this situation as Auto Scaling Group Desynchronization.

4.2. Desynchronization Triggers

Numerous factors can trigger desynchronization in an Auto Scaling Group:

1. **Inaccurate Health Evaluation:** Auto Scaling Groups function based on health checks which evaluate the physical and operational welfare of instances. Inaccurate health status or failed health checks can result in erroneous actions, such as unnecessary terminations or launches.

2. **Inadequate Configuration and Management:** Misconfigured settings or improper group size configuration could lead to instances running either more or less than anticipated. Inconsistencies like tagging failures or not utilizing lifecycle hooks can also cause discrepancies in ASG.

3. **Aggressive Scaling Policies**: Excessive scaling activities on short monitors encourage flapping, a state where the system frequently vacillates between scaling in and scaling out, leading to an inconsistent actual state.

4. **Erroneous Application of Metrics**: Metrics govern the system's response to various conditions. Improper monitoring and wrong metric application can cause unintended scaling activities, propelling the system into an unforeseen state.

5. **Provisioning failures**: Hardware failures or instance type availability issues can cause failed provision attempts, thereby misaligning the ASG's actual state from what is expected.

4.3. Traffic and Load Conditions

A typical Auto Scaling service operates based on key performance metrics such as latency, error rates, CPU, memory, and I/O read/write usage indicators, and more. Inconsistencies in projected metrics or actual traffic trends resulting from application or network issues can instigate unexpected scaling actions leading to ASG desynchronization.

For example, a brief spike in error rates (perhaps due to backend service issues or distributed denial of service (DDoS) attacks) can prompt an unwarranted scaling-out action. Subsequent normalization of the error rate might not immediately scale the system back to its previous state, particularly if the cooldown period configuration is long-lasting, thus resulting in a desynchronized ASG.

4.4. Role of Infrastructure Changes

Modifications in cloud infrastructure, such as network updates or security group adjustments, can impact instance connectivity, leading to perceived unavailability. These infrastructure changes, if not accurately reflected in the ASG configuration, can result in faulty status assessments and unintentional scaling operations.

4.5. Underlying Application Issues

Problems at the application level also contribute to ASG desynchronization. A faulty application could inexplicably consume system resources, triggering scale-out operations unnecessarily. Alternatively, a slow startup application might appear unhealthy due to elongated initialization, causing premature termination and inducing a desynchronized state. Ensuring application healthiness and optimization is essential for effective ASG operation.

4.6. External Dependencies

External dependencies, like database connections or integrated APIs, undergoing unexpected changes, can cause fluctuation in the apps' functional parameters. These variations might trigger unwarranted scale out or scale in operations, leading to ASG desynchronization.

Now that we have explored the potential causes of Auto Scaling Group Desynchronization, we can proceed to the next section outlining preventive measures and solutions. This exploration would offer a deeper understanding of how to manage, counter, and ideally prevent ASG desynchronization, moving toward resilient, efficient, and seamless system operations.

Chapter 5. Impacts of Desynchronization on System Performance

As our systems continue to handle an increasing amount of traffic, the relevance of taking care of the details such as auto scaling group synchronization becomes critical. The impacts of desynchronization are vast and can be detrimental to system performance.

5.1. The Direct Impact on System Scalability

The foundation of any robust and modern system should be its adaptability and scalability, ready to handle spikes in traffic. But what happens when desynchronization affects auto scaling groups? Quite simply, it can cause our systems to fail in delivering the required performance levels during periods of heavy load. Inevitably, each inconsistent group will perform with different efficiency levels, leading to instability throughout the system. This can transform an expected linear growth in resource allocation to a disjointed and unpredictable model, that becomes incredibly challenging to manage.

Desynchronization can cause certain instances within the group to lose their connection with the load balancer, which will not only lead to improper distribution of traffic but also increase the risk of overloading specific instances. This situation can result in decreased scalability, and in worst-case scenarios, system instability or total failure.

5.2. The Impact on System Resilience

Another aspect that faces the brunt of desynchronization's impacts is our system's resilience. Systems are created to adapt and withstand varying traffic loads, ensuring constant and reliable service availability. However, desynchronization can wreak havoc on these resilience capabilities.

There may be instances where a fraction of the group gets detached due to desynchronization, effectively slashing the system's resilience capacity in half. It leaves the system exposed, dramatically decreasing its capability to recover from sudden surges in traffic levels or system failures.

Additionally, during an unexpected system error or failure, recovery processes could be significantly hampered by desynchronization. The reason? Well, desynchronization leads to inconsistencies in the health status of instances within your group, and this makes the orchestration of recovery processes much more complex – and in some cases, nearly impossible.

5.3. Influence on Operational Costs

Desynchronization can also lead to an unexpected increase in overhead and operational costs. When desynchronization occurs, it can cause certain instances to become isolated and underutilized, while others are overburdened. This can not only lead to poor system performance but also mean that you are paying for resources that you aren't optimally utilizing.

Let's say, for instance, that half of your instances become desynchronized and don't share the workload evenly because they are not communicating effectively with the load balancer. In this case, you would still be paying for the idle resources, while also bearing the costs of overused instances, which could include increased wear and tear and earlier-than-expected replacement costs. Therefore, the financial implications of desynchronization can be crucial and should not be overlooked.

5.4. Disruption in Service Availability

Desynchronization can cause severe disruptions in service. When part of your auto scaling group is not in sync, it can disrupt the consistent application of updates, patches, or configurations across the system. This disrupts system harmony and can, in turn, diminish the quality of service provided to users.

In a real-world scenario, consider how disruptive it would be if a user connects to one instance that provides one version of your service, and then their subsequent request is handled by another instance providing a slightly different experience. This kind of unpredictable and inconsistent service could lead to dissatisfaction and even attrition in your user base.

Moreover, with desynchronization, certain instances might not be reported accurately to the load balancer due to erroneous health checks. Hence, they would be incorrectly treated as unavailable, reducing the available services for the users despite these instances being idle.

5.5. The Effect on System Security

Finally, desynchronization doesn't just affect system performance; it can also have grave implications for system security. Imagine a scenario where updates or security patches aren't consistently applied because of auto scaling group desynchronization.

In such situations, desynchronization poses a risk where security updates might not reach every server or instance evenly due to miscommunication, leaving certain instances exposed to security vulnerabilities.

Simply put, if not all instances are updated with the latest security patches because of desynchronization, it gives potential attackers more chances to find weak points in the infrastructure. The system becomes only as strong as its weakest link, a scenario that underlines the urgent need to address the issue of auto scaling group desynchronization.

Each of these outlined impacts projects a crucial aspect of system performance that could be severely affected by auto scaling group desynchronization. It signifies that desynchronization is not a trivial problem, but a vital system issue that directly impacts scalability, resilience, costs, service availability, and security. Hence, it needs to be earnestly understood, analyzed, and addressed by system architects and IT practitioners for building robust, resilient, and efficient systems.

Chapter 6. Red Flags: Identifying the Signs of Desynchronization

As we delve into the crux of the issue, the identification of signs that indicate desynchronization in auto-scaling groups becomes vital. Recognizing these red flags early can help save time and resources, avoiding any potential system inefficiency or downtime. In this section, we don't only alert you to the symptoms but also arm you with the understanding necessary to proactively address the issue.

6.1. The Prelude: Unanticipated Fluctuations

Unpredictable fluctuations may often be the first signs of looming desynchronization. These may be latency spikes, irregular traffic patterns, or sudden changes in the system's load that cannot be efficiently accounted for by conventional scalability. Although traffic surges can also occur due to unforeseen circumstances, persistent patterns may suggest the onset of a desynchronization issue.

```
[NOTE]
====
Keep an eye out on your monitoring and analytics
systems. These irregularities in your metrics may be the
first harbingers of desynchronized auto-scaling groups.
====
```

6.2. Unevenly Distributed Workloads

In optimal circumstances, the workload among instances within an auto-scaling group should be evenly distributed. When desynchronization takes place, this balance is disrupted. It can lead to some instances being overloaded, while others are underutilized. Despite the system scaling, the issue here is that it's not proportionally adjusting to the demand, resulting in uneven workload distribution.

```
[TIP]
====
Frequent audit of your CloudWatch Monitoring Dashboard
(if using AWS) or a similar tool for other cloud
platforms could provide insights into the distribution
of workloads among your instances.
====
```

6.3. Discrepancies in Metrics Reporting

Notification of inconsistent or incorrect system metrics also serve as red flags. Metrics are the vital indicators of system health and are the primary source of information upon which auto-scaling decisions are made. Therefore, discrepancies can lead to erroneous scaling actions which further propagate the desynchronization.

```
[WARNING]
====
Inconsistencies in your metrics data reporting mandate
immediate attention as they may mislead your scaling
```

    policies and trigger unnecessary scalability
    adjustments.
    ====

6.4. Failed Health Checks

Auto-scaling groups normally use health checks to determine the status of instances. If these health checks continuously fail or show inconsistencies for certain instances, it could be a probable sign of desynchronization. While occasional failures can occur due to transient infrastructural or network issues, continuous failures are indicative of deeper systemic problems.

    [IMPORTANT]
    ====
    Maintain a consistent audit of your health check
    reports. These reports can provide valuable insights
    into your system's performance and identify areas of
    potential synchronization loss.
    ====

6.5. Abnormal Auto-scaling Activities

Auto-scaling groups are designed to automatically scale resources based on demand. However, if instances are added or removed erratically, without any corresponding distinct changes in demand or in response to incorrect metrics, these can be potential signs of desynchronization.

    [TIP]
    ====

6.6. Inefficient Use of Resources

An efficient auto-scaling group will ensure optimal resource utilization by scaling up or down as needed. However, in situations where resources are being underutilized or overprovisioned, there could be a potential desynchronization issue at play. It is important to note that, while inefficiencies can occur due to various reasons, persistent inefficiencies could probably signify desynchronization.

[NOTE]
====
Keep a close watch on your resources. If instances are
ideal for long durations, or if there are a high number
of idle resources within your pool, it could be a
symptom of desynchronization in your auto-scaling
groups.
====

In conclusion, it should be noted that these warning signs are often subtle and could be mistaken for minor irregularities. However, early detection and prompt preventive actions can curtail any subsequent major disruptions caused by auto-scaling group desynchronization. By focusing on understanding your auto-scaling environment, monitoring system metrics closely, and keeping an open mind about possible issues, you can ensure that your systems stay synchronized and optimally operational.

Chapter 7. Proactive Measures: Preventing Desynchronization

Without any preliminary ado, let us delve right into the subject matter at hand.

7.1. Understanding Desynchronization

Desynchronization in auto-scaling groups is essentially a disparity between the number of running instances and the expected instances within a group. It is imperative to understand that auto-scaling mechanisms rely on making decisions based on real-time metrics and ideally, the number of running instances should align perfectly with what is desired. When this fails, it leads to ineffective resource utilization and poor service delivery.

See the disparity as a leak in a system – it may start small but has the potential to escalate rapidly, rendering the entire system inefficient, or even worse, inoperable.

7.2. Identifying Potential Causes of Desynchronization

Prior to implementing preventive measures, it's necessary to understand some common scenarios that often lead to desynchronization:

- *Unexpected termination or failure of instances* – This could be due to internal errors within the instance or network issues hampering communication between the instance and the service.

- *Outdated launch configurations* – Rapidly evolving digital landscapes require frequent updates to any system, failure to keep up with these changes could lead to instance launch failures.

- *Over-capacity demands* – If demands spike beyond what the current group can support, you might find some instances failing to launch, leading to desynchronization.

- *Inappropriate load balancing* – Lack of correct load balancing strategies can overburden certain instances causing them to fail, thus causing desynchronization within the group.

- *Faulty health checks* – If the health checks are not configured properly, it might end up failing healthy instances adding to desynchronization troubles.

Now that we have identified potential causes of desynchronization, what are the preventive steps that can be taken?

7.3. The Preventive Approach

"An ounce of prevention is worth a pound of cure" – A timeless proverb that certainly holds in this context. Proactive steps taken to prevent the desynchronization challenge can save a great deal of effort and resources. But how can this be done?

7.4. Keeping Your System Updated

Take time to regularly evaluate your auto-scaling routines, the launch configurations, and other essential elements. Ensuring these are up-to-date implies that they are optimized as per the changing norms and demands. More importantly, it means that they are compliant with the newer and tighter security norms. In consonance with this, auto-scaling groups should be configured to automatically replace instances with outdated launch configurations.

7.5. Ensuring Appropriate Health Checks

Health checks function like silent sentinels, monitoring the system for any red flags. It's important that they are configured correctly and cover a broad spectrum of potential failure points.

Consider employing a combination of health-check mechanisms, both from within the instances and from a third-party observer. A multi-pronged approach can provide a robust method of evaluating instance functionality and performance.

7.6. Effective Load Balancing

Having a competent load balancing strategy can mean the difference between overburdening a handful of instances or evenly distributing tasks. This can enhance group efficiency and significantly reduce the likelihood of instance failures.

Assuring that the load balancer is correctly configured and able to cope with unexpected traffic spikes can prevent potential desynchronization.

7.7. Capacity Planning and Management

Another step towards preventing desynchronization involves appropriate capacity planning and management. The auto-scaling group should be able to handle sudden spikes in traffic or activity. To facilitate this, you can:

- Predict trends and plateaus in your traffic - Machine Learning and predictive analytics can provide invaluable insights.

- Implement a robust and scalable infrastructure - Consider not just your current needs, but your potential needs in the coming years.

This step indeed mitigates not just the risk of desynchronization but improves performance too.

7.8. Regular Audit, Monitor, and Optimize

Last, but certainly not least, regular audits of your auto-scaling groups should be an integral part of your preventive strategy. By maintaining a close eye on your groups, you can spot any inconsistencies or potential issues early.

Monitoring needs to go beyond just resource usage - Start monitoring trends, response times, resource allocation over time, and more. Optimizing based on these insights can lead to not just a stable system, but one which keeps improving.

In conclusion, it is important to remember that the perfect auto-scaling group does not exist. It would change and evolve, sync, and desync, as per the needs of the hour. Despite all preventive measures, there will be some desynchronization – look at it as the system's way of adapting. However, continuous and consistent preventive action can ensure that these are minor blips and not major roadblocks.

Chapter 8. Reactive Strategies: Remediation Techniques for Desynchronization

Auto Scaling Group (ASG) efficacy largely depends on its flawless synchronization. When desynchronization occurs, it can compromise the effective operation of your system. Reactive strategies aim to identify and resolve such issues post-emergence, with the ultimate goal of minimizing their potential impact on system operations.

8.1. Understanding Desynchronization

Desynchronization typically transpires when instances within an ASG are not correctly reporting their states, which can result in operational discrepancies. This generally arises due to connectivity issues, discrepancies in system time, or when an instance fails to boot successfully.

Firstly, it's crucial that all ASG servers maintain an accurate system time. Time synchronization aids in logging and event sequencing, which are immensely critical for fault diagnostics and problem analysis.

Next, we delve into the significance of managing instances that fail to boot correctly. If an instance fails, it's crucial to identify and address this problem swiftly to mitigate the risk of desynchronization.

8.2. Incident Detection and Diagnostics

Incident Detection is the first step towards resolving desynchronization. This involves monitoring your ASG for signs of de-alignment and employing diagnostics tools to define the problem. CloudWatch, AWS's monitoring service, can provide useful insights into the health of your instances and ASG.

Developing a system log is another invaluable tool for incident detection. By keeping a record of each instance's activity, you can review and identify abnormalities.

8.3. Incident Reporting

When an incident is detected, it is essential to have an effective reporting system in place. A detailed incident report should include the time of occurrence, a description of the occurring event, affected components, and initial assumptions about the cause. This information is fundamental in strategizing an appropriate resolution.

8.4. Remediation Techniques

Once an issue has been identified and reported, the next step is remediation. This may require different strategies, depending on the cause and severity of the desynchronization.

1. Time desynchronization: This can often be resolved by employing Network Time Protocol (NTP) to synchronize the system time across all instances.

2. Connectivity issues: If instances are failing to report their states due to connectivity issues, consider revising your networking infrastructure or employing network monitoring tools such as AWS VPC Flow Logs.

3. Boot failures: If instances are failing to boot, then a possible remedy could be to replace the affected instances. This could be achieved through the automatic replacement of unhealthy instances, a feature offered by AWS Auto Scaling.

8.5. Post-Remediation Review

Following the implementation of the prescribed remediation technique, it's critical to review the system to confirm the successful resolution of the issue. This check ensures that the applied resolution is working as expected and prevents possible recurring issues.

8.6. Prescription of Proactive Measures

While reactive strategies are crucial in managing ASG desynchronization as they occur, they should be complemented with preventative strategies. Employing monitoring tools, regularly reviewing system status, and maintaining a detailed log of incident reports can significantly reduce the potential for desynchronization.

To conclude, managing ASG desynchronization effectively involves a calculated blend of problem diagnosis, insightful incident reporting, strategic remediation, and careful post-remediation review. A proactive approach, combined with an effective reactive strategy, can ensure the robustness of your auto-scaling groups and save valuable time and resources in maintaining system synchronized operations.

Chapter 9. Case Study: Real-World Desynchronization Issues and Their Solutions

In our first encounter with the issue of desynchronization, we were brought onboard to troubleshoot a mature application that had been running seamlessly for several years. However, the customer had begun reporting sporadic and unexplained system failures. These system failures led to multiple service disruptions, impacting both productivity and revenues. The application was complex, comprising of multiple Auto Scaling Groups (ASGs) that had been architected to support periods of unpredictable customer demand.

9.1. The Initial Investigation

We started with an in-depth analysis of the metrics provided by Amazon CloudWatch, looking at the application logs, dumpster diving into the torrent of data in search of anomalies. Two primary areas caught our attention: high service latencies and occasional network timeouts. But the root cause remained elusive. The system appeared to be working as designed, scaling in and out based on demand, with no visible discrepancies in the configurations. There was nothing, it seemed, that explained these unexpected performance degradations.

The breakthrough arrived when we correlated events from the ELB (Elastic Load Balancer) logs and EC2 instance logs. During periods of peak customer demand, instances were being created and terminated at a rapid rate in response to increased load. But here was the catch: after every scale-in event, the ELB continued to route client requests to instances that had been terminated. This situation, known as a phantom instance problem, was clearly identified as the culprit.

9.2. The Phantom Instance Problem

A closer dive into the issue revealed that the ASG controller did not notify the ELB about instance termination until it received a confirmation from the instance itself. However, due to the abrupt nature of termination, instances were taken out of rotation before they had a chance to update the ELB about their status. The ELB, in turn, was unaware of this termination and continued to route client requests to the nonexistent instance, leading to network timeout and failures.

The phantom instance problem essentially encompassed ASG's and ELB's inability to stay synchronized in real-time during rapid scale-in events, which resulted in the desynchronization problem we were witnessing.

9.3. Implementing the Solution

Our solution to mitigate this problem was to harmonize the ASG and ELB, ensuring that the ELB was aware of the instances' status in real-time. We replaced the default termination policy of ASG with a custom Lambda function. This function would deregister the instance from the ELB before termination, giving us an opportunity to drain connections gracefully at the same time.

```
The Lambda function code snippet:

[source,python]
```

```python
import boto3 def lambda_handler(event, context): instance_id = event['detail']['EC2InstanceId'] asg = boto3.client('autoscaling') response = asg.describe_auto_scaling_instances(InstanceIds=[instance_id]) elb = boto3.client('elbv2') elb.deregister_targets(TargetGroupArn='<Target-
```

Group-ARN>', Targets=[{'Id': instance_id}])

Simply put, with this new approach, we informed the ELB that a certain instance was going off the grid. After deregistration, we provided a cool-down period for the instance to process any pending requests, post which the instance was terminated.

9.4. Verifying the Improvement

Following the implementation of the updated Lambda function, the occurrence of phantom instances was virtually eliminated. The client reported a marked decrease in latency, and most significantly, fewer network timeouts. Ultimately, system stability was restored, and the recurring service disruptions were all but a distant memory.

It's worth noting that while this solution resolved the particular issue at hand, ASG-ELB desynchronization can exhibit itself in a variety of forms. It's not always confined to the problem of phantom instances. Nevertheless, the strategies of careful observation, precise analysis, apt problem definition, and tailored solution-building apply to all such scenarios.

Chapter 10. Future-Proofing: Ensuring Long-Term System Robustness

Maintaining the long-term robustness of your system necessitates a strong understanding of foundational principles, continuous evaluation, and future-proofing. Broadly speaking, this involves consistently identifying and mitigating the potential risks of Auto Scaling Group Desynchronization and employing measures to assure system sustainability.

10.1. Understanding the Foundations

In configuring auto scaling groups, it's critical to grasp the principles that underpin their functionality. This understanding, in turn, elevates your capability to troubleshoot any unprecedented issues as well as future-proof systems.

Auto Scaling Groups (ASGs) maintain a fleet of instances and regulate their quantity according to the demand. They work as a pivotal component of resilient architectures, ensuring optimal resource allocation, maximizing availability and minimizing costs.

However, these ASGs can fall into a desynchronized state, creating disparities between the desired and actual system states. Consequently, it can lead to overprovisioning or underprovisioning of resources, lofty expenses, and possible system downtime—issues prone to escalate over time if not appropriately managed.

10.2. Evaluating and Mitigating Risks

Frequent and consistent evaluation of your ASG state is fundamental in preempting desynchronization issues. Through regular monitoring, you can identify potential triggers, risks, and unfavorable patterns before they fully materialize.

Identifying irregularities early enough gives you a formidable advantage in curbing these issues. Moreover, keeping a well-documented record of all system changes and modifications can come handy in resolving potential discrepancies.

Operational costs surge when instances remain idle due to overprovisioning, whereas underprovisioning can result in inadequate performance or possible system failure. Addressing either scenario involves tuning the ASG configurations correctly. Properly created and timed scaling policies are critical, based on carefully determined and evaluated thresholds regarding metrics such as CPU utilization, network usage, or custom metrics configured by the system admin.

10.3. Real-Time Monitoring and Alerting Systems

Investing in competent real-time monitoring tools is crucial. These tools provide vital insights into the system's current state, enabling prompt detection of anomalies. You can use these insights to create alerting policies for events that might lead to desynchronization.

Alerting systems notify the relevant teams whenever thresholds breach, allowing immediate attention. This way, your team can resolve minor hiccups promptly before morphing into serious issues, thereby maintaining a healthy system state.

10.4. Embracing Automation

Automation is a friend of future-proofing. In auto scaling, automation can help maintain consistency, reduce human error, and offer far-reaching cost and time efficiencies. Automating tasks such as health checks, automatic replacement of faulty instances, and re-syncing operations will keep the system running smoothly without manual supervision.

10.5. Holistic Testing

Automated testing forms an integral part of system robustness. Develop tests that mimic real-life scenarios to validate the performance and anticipated behaviors of your systems. Such testing can identify weak points and discrepancies, enabling preemptive troubleshooting.

10.6. Regular System Upgrades and Patches

Regular system upgrades and patches play a significant role in maintaining the system's overall health. Every new version commonly involves enhancements and fixes that can prevent impending issues or plug vulnerabilities. Hence, ensure that system components are updated at all times.

10.7. Designing for Failures

Account for failures by setting up redundant components in the system to safeguard against systematic errors and hardware failures. Plan for failure scenarios and establish countermeasures. Incorporate concepts like Chaos Engineering to simulate failures and observe how systems behave.

10.8. Knowledge Sharing and Up-to-Date Documentation

Lastly, maintaining up-to-date documentation and organizing regular knowledge sharing sessions among the team can help identify potential risks in advance. These sessions offer everyone an opportunity to share ideas, learn, and foster rapid solutions to emerging challenges.

In building future-proof systems, it's crucial to remember that long-term robustness doesn't invariably mean preventing issues. Instead, it involves developing mechanisms for detecting and resolving issues promptly and minimizing their impact. Adopting these measures translates to enduring, resilient, and optimized operations, safeguarding against Auto Scaling Group Desynchronization.

Chapter 11. Conclusion: Moving Forward with Optimized Auto Scaling Groups

After an extensive exploration of the challenges, causes, solutions, and preventative measures regarding Auto Scaling Group Desynchronization, it's time to reflect upon key points and project a way forward for optimized Auto Scaling Groups (ASGs). This conclusion serves as a summary of our in-depth discussion with hopes of empowering you to maintain seamless and resilient system operations.

11.1. Unraveling the Core Topic

Recall that at the heart of our discussion lies the concept of Auto Scaling Groups, integral to a cloud computing environment. Their role is pivotal in maintaining system availability and elasticity without manual intervention. However, we discussed how this great advantage could be marred by a phenomenon we refer to as "desynchronization".

Understanding how desynchronization occurs is the first stepping stone towards rectifying it. Desynchronization in Auto Scaling Groups tends to occur when the state of ASGs fail to align with the real-time requirement of instances. This could be due to unexpected failures, glitches or manual interventions.

11.2. Consequences of Desynchronization

Desynchronization has severe implications. It leads to a lack of resource optimization, resulting in unnecessarily inflated costs, increased chances of failures, and decreased overall system reliability. This makes recognizing the signs of desynchronization crucial.

Recognition comes from increased visibility. Developing efficient logging and auditing systems will be paramount in identifying the exact issues causing desynchronization.

11.3. Rectifying and Preventing Desynchronization

Moving on, we discussed the suitable actions towards resolving this problem. It included a broad spectrum of solutions ranging from manual dissipation of the mismatch to automated solutions such as scripting and predefined templates.

The application of Infrastructure-as-Code (IaC) practices for the configuration and deployment of ASGs can help ensure consistency and traceability, significantly mitigating the risk of desynchronization.

Then, we navigated through preventive measures. The notion of 'keeping things tracked' surfaced numerous times in our discussion. Following a robust change management process, doing frequent audits and establishing activity alarms were amongst the recommended measures to prevent desynchronization in ASGs.

11.4. Embracing the Future

Looking to the future, as technology progresses and cloud computing environments continue to grow and evolve, so must our approaches to managing and optimizing them. It's crucial to harness machine learning and artificial intelligence to predict patterns, recognize anomalies, and streamline the process of re-synchronization.

Additionally, embrace software as a service (SaaS) and platform as a service (PaaS) offerings. These services can help manage ASGs, ensure optimal performance, and prevent desynchronization, freeing up resources to focus on development and innovation tasks.

11.5. Keeping Up with Technology

With advancements in technology, building sophisticated, reliable, and maintainable systems becomes increasingly possible. Despite this, it's fundamental to remember that the eloquence of a system lies not in its complexity, but in its ability to function effectively and to recover quickly from potential failures.

Stay in the loop with advances in the fields of Distributed Systems, DevOps, and AI in addition to keeping your knowledge on ASG and cloud computing up-to-date. Regularly revisiting your strategies for managing ASGs is equally important in order to embrace new technologies and methods that might prove beneficial.

In conclusion, knowing about Auto Scaling Group Desynchronization and its consequences is just half of the story. The other half, arguably the more essential one, is gaining the ability to prepare, prevent, rectify, adapt, and evolve. With ASGs forming the backbone of modern, distributed systems, understanding and taking measures to prevent desynchronization will greatly enhance the integrity, resilience, and efficiency of your entire system.

We hope this report equips you with a robust understanding of the issue at hand. As you move forward, guided by this resource, we wish you a more seamless experience in managing and optimizing your Auto Scaling Groups.